LOHFELD
CONSULTING
GROUP, INC.

Best Informed Wins
Volume 2

Collected Articles of
Bob Lohfeld from
Washington Technology
2013 – 2015

Edited by Beth Wingate

LOHFELD
CONSULTING
GROUP, INC.

Best Informed Wins
Volume 2

Collected Articles of
Bob Lohfeld from
Washington Technology
2013 – 2015

Edited by Beth Wingate

Articles reprinted with permission from
WashingtonTechnology.com
Printed in United States of America
ISBN: 978-0-9887554-5-1

Published by Lohfeld Consulting Group, Inc.
940 South River Landing Road
Edgewater, Maryland 21037

For more information, contact Info@LohfeldConsulting.com
Production and copyediting: Alexandra Wingate and Beth Wingate

| Dedication

Many thanks to Nick Wakeman, Editor-in-Chief of *WashingtonTechnology.com* for your continuing support and dedication to our government contracting industry.

Best Informed Wins

Volume 2 – Collected Articles of Bob Lohfeld
from *Washington Technology* (2013 – 2015)

Contents

Best Informed Wins

Volume 2 – Collected Articles of Bob Lohfeld
from *Washington Technology* (2013 – 2015)

5 questions to derail an LPTA procurement

*What you ask might guide an agency
away from a low-price contract*

While teaching a capture management class, a capture manager asked me what he could do when the contracting officer for a pending IT services bid said he wanted to use lowest price technically acceptable (LPTA) evaluation criteria versus the traditional best-value tradeoff approach.

The capture manager and the government program manager wanted to avoid a price shootout, but the contracting shop wouldn't agree.

When confronted with this situation, here are five questions a capture manager should answer to help the technical client steer clear of LPTA requirements.

Best Informed Wins

Volume 2 – Collected Articles of Bob Lohfeld
from *Washington Technology* (2013 – 2015)

1. Does the use of LPTA violate government guidance?

Does your client know that the Defense Department (DOD) has a policy statement providing guidance on when to use LPTA evaluation criteria instead of the best-value approach that trades off cost and non-cost factors? *Appendix A* of the DOD's *Source Selection Procedure* (3/4/11) (http://goo.gl/6g7145) contains the policy and states that, "LPTA may be used in situations where the government would not realize any value from a proposal exceeding the government's minimum technical or performance requirements, often for acquisitions of commercial or non-complex services or supplies which are clearly defined and expected to be low risk."

If your services are complex or if poor performance could expose the agency to unacceptable risk, then using the LPTA evaluation criteria would be inappropriate.

FAR 15.101-2 (a) provides a similar statement for LPTA bids, "The lowest price technically acceptable source selection process is appropriate when best value is expected to result from selection of the technically acceptable proposal with the lowest evaluated price."

When using LPTA, the government must accept that there is no benefit from an offeror exceeding a contract requirement rather than just barely meeting it. Consequently, the only judgment an evaluator can render is that the offer meets the minimum requirements or it doesn't. This means the government must accept a marginally capable bidder and grant that bidder the same standing as the best, most innovative firms in the industry. This is often an unacceptable position when the government strives to achieve service or technical excellence.

2. Can you define technical acceptability?

DOD provides additional guidance in its *Better Buying Power 2.0 Memorandum to the Defense Acquisition Workforce* (11/13/12) (http://goo.gl/Of0vIk). This guidance states, "Industry has expressed concerns about the use of Lowest Price, Technically Acceptable (LPTA) selection criteria that essentially defaults to the

lowest price bidder, independent of quality.
Where LPTA is used, the Department needs to
define [technically acceptable] appropriately to
ensure adequate quality."

The procurement office should defer to the
technical team for guidance on what constitutes
technical acceptability. For procurements
involving software development, systems
integration, systems engineering, solution
architecture, etc., it is hard enough to define the
work let alone the criteria for technical
acceptability. If the government cannot specify
what constitutes technical acceptability in the RFP,
then the procurement should not use LPTA
selection criteria.

3. Is past performance important?

If past performance is important to the buyer, then
LPTA may not be an acceptable evaluation
criterion. The guidance from DOD states that, "In
the case of an offeror without a record of relevant
past performance or for whom information on
past performance is not available or so sparse that
no meaningful past performance rating can be

reasonably assigned, the offeror may not be evaluated favorably or unfavorably on past performance (see FAR 15.305 (a)(2)(iv)). Therefore, the offeror shall be determined to have unknown past performance. In the context of acceptability/ unacceptability, "unknown" shall be considered "acceptable."

In accordance with the FAR, "If the contracting officer documents the file pursuant to 15.304(c)(3)(iii), past performance need not be an evaluation factor in lowest price technically acceptable source selections."

Guidance from the FAR and DOD allows bidders with no relevant past performance to be treated as though they have the same past performance as the most experienced firms in the industry. If you believe past performance is a predictor of future results, then you may want to steer clear of LPTA evaluation criteria.

4. Is there public opposition to the use of LPTA?

Can you cite articles from the trade press that support your position that LPTA is inappropriate for most IT services procurements? If you

Google *Lowest Price Technically Acceptable*, you can find 50 articles that discuss why LPTA should not be used for services bids. If this were my procurement, I would do the search and then send copies of relevant articles to the government technical team and their procurement office. Perhaps the power of the press can turn some folks away from using LPTA inappropriately.

5. Is there a record of failed contract performance?

Can you find evidence of similar service contracts awarded using LPTA evaluation criteria where the contract was either terminated for poor performance or substantially modified to grant price relief to the lowest priced offer? There is much speculation that the inappropriate use of LPTA criteria will ultimately result in contracts with unacceptable performance. If you can document some of these instances, it will strengthen your argument to avoid the LPTA approach.

If you have other strategies to help your customers steer clear of LPTA evaluation criteria and you want to share them, or if you can cite LPTA contracts that have failed, please email your comments to *RLohfeld@LohfeldConsulting.com* so that we can have an open dialog on the misuse of LPTA evaluation criteria.

WashingtonTechnology.com, December 19, 2012

4 strategies that can kill your recompete

*Love is not an evaluation criterion
in federal procurements*

I regularly get calls to review capture strategies for companies competing on *must win* procurements. I have done an equal number of these reviews for companies during the time when they were in their capture phase (before the final request for proposals is released), during their proposal development phase when everyone was working hard to write the winning proposal, and, regrettably, after the company had submitted its proposal and been told that they had lost their *must win* deal.

Often these procurements are for contract recompetes, where the company is the incumbent contractor performing the work. There is a common thread among all of these reviews— incumbent contractors all too often focus on the wrong strategies. I thought I would share some of these losing strategies with you in the hope that you don't take your next *must win* recompete down the same losing path.

1. They love us

Every incumbent contractor, with the possible exception of those who have received multiple cure notices, believes the customer loves them. To reinforce their belief, they argue that they have been performing the work satisfactorily day in and day out for years, and there have been no loud complaints from the customer about their performance. Silence in this case is mistaken for love.

The more they convince themselves that the customer loves them, the more complacent they become in how they perform the work, and the more resistant they become to changes in how they propose to do the work. All companies who fall victim to this belief will eventually discover that love is not an evaluation criterion in federal procurements. The sooner they set aside the belief that what they are doing today is good enough,

the sooner they will get serious about creating
better ways to do the work.

2. Fear, uncertainty, and doubt (FUD)

Another incumbent shortcoming is to believe they
are the only contractor who can perform the work,
and should the government change contractors,
the successor contractor would be unable to
recruit the incumbent staff needed to perform the
contract. Incumbents echo this strategy
throughout their proposals by repeatedly using
the phrase, "As the incumbent contractor, we are
the low-risk provider of these services." The
incumbent tries to raise the specter of fear,
uncertainty, and doubt (FUD) in the minds of the
evaluators, hoping this will serve as justification
for the government to keep them in place for the
next 5 years.

You cannot imagine how annoying this statement
can become to government evaluators. The
government knows well that you are the
incumbent, and they know transition can bring
some risk. However, contracts are transitioned
every day from one contractor to another, and the

world goes on without missing a beat. Evaluators are told that being the incumbent contractor is not a justification for award and will ignore such statements. These statements just take up valuable proposal space that could be used to say something worthwhile. Annoying your evaluator is not a win strategy, and incumbents should delete or minimize these statements from their proposals.

3. Looking in the rear view mirror

I was once told that you should never let your project team write the proposal for its recompete. While I don't completely agree with that statement, there is some truth in it. For example, I watched one project team respond to every question in the RFP by describing in detail what they had done for their customer over the past 5 years. It was a wonderful history lesson, but a history lesson is not a proposal. A proposal is about what you are going to do going forward, not what you did in the past. You don't drive a car forward by looking in the rear view mirror, and you should not write your proposal by filling it with what you did in the past. Look forward, embrace the future, and stop clinging to the past.

4. Ignoring your competition

Every non-incumbent challenger uses the same two-pronged strategy to take work away from an incumbent.

First, they argue that the incumbent uses outdated processes, procedures, and tools to do the work and that their solution is antiquated and not current with today's technology. The challenger offers to bring better processes, procedures, solutions, etc. when selected to perform the contract. Their proposal will be rich in features showing newer, better approaches than those the incumbent has been using, and they will argue that these bring additional value to the government.

Second, they will argue that the incumbent has let costs get out of control by allowing salaries to creep beyond current market rates and indirect costs to escalate. They will offer to perform the work for less cost and will justify these statements by proposing tighter indirect rates and bringing new, less-expensive people into the workforce to lower overall costs.

As the incumbent, you must counter these threats and create a strategy to prevent the challengers from taking the contract away. The best counter is for you also to bring innovative ideas to the workforce and to reduce your proposed costs. To do otherwise would be to give your competition the upper hand.

Understand the value of incumbency

Incumbency is a wonderful thing. It gives you the high ground from which you can see more clearly what your customer wants over the next term of your contract and, with that insight, you should be able to craft a winning offer that will deliver just what your customer wants.

Incumbency doesn't make you the next winner— it's what you do with that incumbency that makes the difference.

WashingtonTechnology.com, January 30, 2013

Can you hire an effective capture manager?

Three tips for finding the right person

The CEO of a mid-tier company asked me why many capture managers turn out to be ineffective and, in his case, could he have done something differently in the interview process to predict their effectiveness before hiring them.

This is a difficult question because most capture managers will interview well, but some will not live up to expectations once on the job. I thought I would share some insights about this situation.

The triple threat

Capture managers are part business development (BD) manager, part project manager, and part proposal manager. In this hybrid role, they serve to prepare a company to compete for and win the larger, more-complex bids in the government market and are appointed when a company makes a decision to pursue a particular procurement.

You should view capture managers as a triple threat—professionals who are skilled in the three areas of BD, project management, and proposal management and can lead any and all of these areas.

Capture managers act like BD managers when they interface with prospective customers to gather a deeper understanding of customer needs, requirements, and objectives. Additionally, they must be keenly aware of other competitors—and their strengths and weaknesses—and lead your efforts to develop your win strategy. They must understand the dynamics of the government market and be able to shape the procurement in a way that is advantageous to your firm. Capture managers are your company's spokesperson when talking with the customer, and they represent your firm in all external matters related to the pursuit of their assigned procurement.

Capture managers also act like project managers. They lead your company's exercise to develop your technical and managerial solutions that (hopefully) are rich in features that will separate your firm from your competition. They select the personnel you propose to staff the project and your teaming partners and subcontractors, establish your bid price, and minimize risk to your firm should you be awarded the project.

Finally, capture managers act as proposal managers by overseeing your proposal development effort with the proposal manager reporting directly to them. To do this effectively, the capture manager must drive the proposal, integrating your solution into the proposal by skillfully placing features of your solution into the right sections of the proposal where they will get the greatest score and ensuring that your proposal communicates your solution effectively to the customer.

You should view capture managers as a triple threat—professionals who are skilled in the three areas of BD, project management, and proposal management and can lead any and all of these areas.

Capture manager prerequisites

To be an effective capture manager, you need experience and skills in BD, project management, and proposal management. I believe you should have served at some point in your career in each of these roles. Being familiar with proposal management and being able to lead it are worlds apart. Similarly, being able to understand the technical areas your firm works in and being the external spokesperson for your company in these areas in discussions with the prospective customer are, again, different ends of the same technical spectrum.

So often, we see companies force fitting people into the capture manager role and then justifying the selection by saying, "Meeting all prerequisites is not necessary." I have heard company executives say their capture managers don't need to have a good command of their company's technology. They argue that they are a big company with lots of technical wizards, so the capture manager doesn't have to lead this area.

When they say this, what they are really doing is rationalizing their decision to put less-qualified persons into the role of capture manager. In modern psychology, this is called cognitive dissonance where the company executive lowers the importance of one of the discordant factors — in this case technical understanding. I'm sure there are some exceptional capture managers who are not technically proficient, but they are the exception, and this should not be the norm for which your company strives.

When interviewing capture managers, establish your prerequisites, and then take the interviewee deeply into discussions in each area. It only takes a few minutes to tell the difference between someone who has real skills in each area and someone who just tosses around the words. Find out how deep their skills are in each prerequisite area and then, if you hire them, know that they are going to need additional skills training in areas where they are weak.

Capture manager leadership skills

Great capture managers have great leadership skills, and they are naturally driven to win. They command the respect of their customers, their peers, and their superiors. They lead through their intellectual skills and have the ability to motivate others around them.

Capture managers lead deals of all different sizes and complexities. When you interview a capture manager, try to understand the complexity and competitive landscape of their past captures. Here dollar size is not a good indicator of capture accomplishment. For some captures, it seems like every competitor wins, and the capture is little more than having the company submit a capability proposal. For others, the capture campaign was complex, the deal was competed fiercely among the top companies in the industry, and only one company came out as the winner.

When you interview prospective capture managers, find out what deals they *led*, not just were *involved with*. Find out what their roles were and what they contributed personally to the effort. Everyone involved with a win will take credit for it. Your job in the interview process is to find out what they really did. I talked with one capture manager who told me how he led his company to fame on a major recompete. As we talked more, I learned that his company had been the incumbent for 16 years, and the government had tried to sole source the procurement to them, but couldn't get it done. They then issued the procurement through a contract vehicle with limited competition and made the award to his firm. In retrospect, he seemed to have contributed little to this pursuit other than having made some corporate briefing charts.

Striving for top capture managers

Capture is an intellectual competition played by the best and brightest people in our industries, and the company that assembles the best team and competes the hardest will most likely win. Capture managers are the quarterback of your team and have to lead your BD, technical, and proposal teams in your campaign to win. If you compromise your standards for capture managers, you will compromise your results.

WashingtonTechnology.com, February 22, 2013

Why some companies embrace LPTA contracts

Lower barrier to entry means marginally credible firms have a shot at winning procurements

Some companies are actively seeking lowest price, technically acceptable (LPTA) professional services bids—but they're not the companies you'd think. You'd expect companies with deep experience in their fields that have honed their operating costs to the minimum and are operating at maximum efficiency to seek out LPTA bids where they could compete on price—but it is just the opposite.

Inexperienced, marginally credible firms are finding that LPTA procurements provide a unique opportunity to penetrate government market segments that they would otherwise have been unable to enter. Here's how it works.

LPTA lowers the barrier to entry

Under LPTA bids, the government awards contracts to offerors with minimally acceptable technical proposals rather than to offers with the best technical proposals as is normally done in best value trade-off procurements.

In other words, the LPTA evaluation criteria provide no additional value to the market leader company over the market laggard company. To pass the test of technical acceptability, a company merely has to squeak over the hurdle of minimal acceptability, and it doesn't matter whether the company squeaks over the hurdle by an inch or clears it by a mile. The evaluation score is the same. All technically acceptable proposals receive the same passing score.

This creates a disadvantage for the best companies in the market that normally compete on their technical superiority. LPTA bids neutralize the competitive advantage of technical superiority because there is no additional value in having a superior technical proposal.

LPTA procurements encourage companies that can only write a marginally credible proposal to bid since they only need to meet the minimum acceptability level and nothing more. The net effect is that these procurements let minimally qualified companies compete on the same technical footing as the best companies in the field.

This lowers the barrier to market entry and allows minimally qualified companies to enter markets that they could have never have competed in before.

LPTA waives the requirement for past performance

Additionally, under LPTA bids, the government will waive the requirement that the offeror demonstrate relevant, successful past performance.

Most LPTA solicitations require the offeror to provide contract references demonstrating successful performance of contracts with similar size, scope, and complexity. In the event the offeror has no record of past performance, or for offerors for whom the record of past performance is not available or is so sparse that no meaningful past performance rating can be assigned, the government will not evaluate the offeror favorably or unfavorably on past performance.

Instead, the offeror will be determined to have unknown past performance. In the context of acceptability/unacceptability in an LPTA bid, unknown is considered acceptable, and a passing score will be awarded for the past performance evaluation factor.

This further lowers the barrier to entry, letting companies with no past performance compete with the same past performance score as market leaders maintaining unblemished past performance records.

Using LPTA to enter new markets

The net effect is that LPTA procurements lower the barrier to market entry, thereby allowing companies with minimally acceptable technical proposals and limited or no past performance to buy into markets they could never enter previously.

As a market-entry strategy, LPTA works well for outsiders to gain a foothold they would otherwise have no chance of gaining.

WashingtonTechnology.com, April 8, 2013

Can you afford to chase premium price? Maybe.

Analysis shows the risk is worth the reward

When the government awards a contract to someone other than the lowest priced offeror, it pays a price premium to make that award. How much price premium the government will pay is left to the judgment of the selecting official. This amount varies by type of service or product being procured, details of each solicitation, and experience of the source selection official (SSO).

In 1999, the price premium in a Government Accountability Office (GAO) study averaged about 7%. In 2010, the price premium in another GAO study averaged about 5%. Today, in the middle of the sequestration battle, the price premium is probably less than that; however, it's difficult to generalize because the price premium can be unique to individual procurements. Here's what we learned from the GAO studies and how you can apply this to your capture strategy.

GAO studies

In October 2010, GAO published a report, *Enhanced Training Could Strengthen DOD's Best Value Tradeoff Decisions* (GAO-11-8) (http://goo.gl/PwPPnJ). In the report, GAO reviewed 68 best-value contract awards made by Defense Department agencies. In the sample of 68 procurements, 42% (29 out of 68) were awarded to the highest rated offerors who also had the lowest price. This is where most bidders want to be—the number one rated proposal and the lowest price.

For the remaining 39 bids, the government conducted a best-value tradeoff. In those instances where the price premium was 5% or less, 92% (12 out of 13) of the awards were made to the highest rated offer.

As the price premium increased, the chance of receiving the award decreased. When the price premium increased above 5%, but was less than 20%, the award was made to the highest rated offeror 53% of the time (7 out of 13). When the price premium exceeded 20%, only 15% of the bidders (2 out of 13) received the award.

The GAO sample of 68 procurements was not selected randomly from DOD awards, so it would be statistically inappropriate to draw sweeping conclusions from their data. Even so, it is tempting to generalize that half the best-value awards go to the offeror with the highest rated/lowest price score. When the government conducted a best-value tradeoff, about 54% of the time the award was made to the highest rated offer, and 46% of the time it was awarded to the lowest priced offeror. When the price premium was within 5%, the offeror had a 92% chance of winning. However, when the price premium increased above 5%, the probability of win dropped to 53%, and above 20% the probability of win dropped to only 15%.

In April 1999, GAO published another study entitled *Acquisition Reform – Review of Best Value Procurements* (B-281983) (http:/goo.gl/ZQzlQ9). In this older study, GAO reviewed 250 procurements covering 37 procuring organizations. Again, the contracts were not selected randomly, so results should not be generalized to all buying organizations across the government.

Of these contracts, 53 (21%) were awarded to offerors who were not the lowest priced offeror because the selecting official believed these companies offered the best value. The 53 contracts had a combined value of $5.3 billion and a price premium, defined as the difference between the awardee's evaluated price and that of the lowest priced acceptable offeror, of $367 million—or a price premium of about 7%. The majority of these contracts were for sophisticated government services and products.

The tradeoff between non-cost and cost factors often cited the offeror's superior technical ability, exceptional management practices, outstanding relevant experience, and ability to meet technical requirements within statutory timeframes because of superior relevant experience. GAO noted that the justification for award to the higher priced offerors was documented in the contract files, and buyers complied with the laws and Federal Acquisition Regulations (FAR) in making these awards.

Best Informed Wins

Volume 2 – Collected Articles of Bob Lohfeld
from *Washington Technology* (2013 – 2015)

Setting your strategy

Most government procurements are competed using a best-value approach. In these cases, the solicitation must state whether non-cost factors are significantly more important, equally important, or less important than price. The exception to this is lowest price technically acceptable (LPTA) procurements. In these instances, there is no best-value tradeoff because the government has determined that offers will be evaluated as either acceptable or not acceptable, and there is no additional value for exceeding solicitation minimum requirements.

In best-value tradeoff procurements, the selecting official must trade off the non-cost factors such as past performance, technical approach, management approach, small business subcontracting plan, and company experience with price. Technical and/or past performance are most often the top evaluation factors. To be the highest rated offeror, you must strive to have an outstanding proposal—one that is rich in features that will be scored as proposal strengths (see my

article on *7 Steps from Good to Great Proposals*)
(http://goo.gl/hBByB6).

From a strategy point of view, you want your
proposal to be the highest rated, and you want
your bid to be the lowest acceptable price or be
within 5% of that amount, otherwise the odds start
lining up against you for receiving the award.

Here's an example of how this might apply to
your bid. Suppose you're bidding a best-value
procurement for $100 million. You decide that you
could write a pretty good proposal, but if you
spent another $100,000 on the proposal, you could
make it outstanding.

If you had an outstanding proposal, you would
probably be in the zone where the selecting official
is looking at your proposal and trading it off
against price. If you are within 5% of the lowest
bid, you have a pretty good chance of winning.
That 5% is worth $5 million on this procurement.

Would you spend an extra $100,000 to buy $5
million of price protection that the bid will not go
to another bidder whose price is less than yours?

Best Informed Wins

Volume 2 – Collected Articles of Bob Lohfeld
from *Washington Technology* (2013 – 2015)

Without trying to be self-serving, I would do it every time.

Your win strategy is get the price right and spend the money to have an outstanding proposal.

WashingtonTechnology.com, May 3, 2013

5 steps to winning proposals

The technical team plays crucial role

I'm amazed at how few companies present good, compelling technical solutions in their proposals. The reason is probably that their technical teams don't know what constitutes a good proposal solution.

In this article, I'm going to describe the process we use to ensure we develop solutions that will score well when reviewed by government proposal evaluators. Here's how we do it.

Step 1 – Understand the requirement

The first step in engineering is to understand the requirement. I don't mean to speak down to you since this seems pretty obvious, but I've read a lot of proposals where the technical team misunderstood the requirement or misinterpreted the intent of the government's RFP.

To make sure everyone understands the requirement, we do a structured walkthrough of the requirement with the technical team. We discuss what is in the statement of work (SOW), the relevant attachments to the RFP, the proposal instructions, and the proposal evaluation criteria.

Let's also make sure we agree on what is not part of the requirement. As engineers might say, "Let's bound the problem." Otherwise, our solution will become open ended and risk not addressing what is important to the evaluators. The better we understand the requirement, the more likely we are to create a winning technical solution.

Step 2 – Create candidate technical solutions

Next, let's look at various technical solutions or approaches to doing the work. We like to have more than one approach since we want to trade off the merits of each as we close in on our preferred solution. The chosen solution should be technically sound, complete, logical, and internally consistent. In other words, we need an excellent technical solution that achieves what the customer has asked for, addresses the appropriate requirements in the RFP, and has no weaknesses in its approach.

Keep the alternative solutions handy since we may want to discuss them in our proposal as alternatives we considered when developing our technical solution, but discarded because our chosen approach is superior. This tradeoff discussion can be an effective way of ghosting another bidder's approach, especially if they have chosen to propose one of the alternative approaches that we discarded.

Step 3 – Engineer in your proposal evaluation strengths

When the government evaluates your technical approach, they will be looking for *proposal strengths*. These are the features of your solution that either 1) increase the likelihood of successful contract accomplishment or 2) exceed a contract requirement in a way that is beneficial to the government. There may be other features that are evaluated as proposal strengths depending on the mission of the agency, for example, lethality of the system, safety inherent in your solution, etc.

Make sure you agree on how the government is going to define proposal strengths. In our experience, the definition is pretty narrow and may cause a lot of the features of your solution to be noted as interesting, but not scored as *proposal strengths.*

As a solution development team, we must comb through your technical solution and identify all features that might be scored as strengths since these will need to be highlighted in your proposal. If we don't find evaluation strengths in your solution, then we go back and rework the solution until we have engineered features into the solution that can be scored as proposals strengths. The more strengths, the better the proposal will score.

For each proposed evaluation strength, make sure you include evidence to support your claims, and clearly delineate the benefit of each feature to ensure that the benefit tracks with the definition of what proposal strengths are for your solution.

Step 4 – Bring in the innovation

There is a natural tension between the need to propose proven solutions and the need to continually improve the way you propose to perform the work being bid. If you are justifying your solution by saying, "This is the way we always do this work," or "This is how we did it last time," then challenge your engineers to do it better, quicker, and cheaper.

Build innovation into your solution and show the government that you are indeed committed to improving the way work is done—and offer real solutions to do this. Make creativity part of your solutioning process, and always remember that last year's breakthrough in technology can become this year's obsolete solution.

Step 5 – Reduce the cost

Challenge your technical team to engineer cost avoidance and cost reduction into their solutions. If it cost you a certain amount to do this work last time, then figure out how you can do it for less. Be mindful that you need to engineer cost reductions into your solution or technical approach when you are creating it, not wait for executive management to force it into your proposal in the final days of the pricing exercise.

Make these five steps part of your solutioning process, and you will consistently produce technical solutions that score well—hopefully bringing you more victories!

WashingtonTechnology.com, August 6, 2013

2014 realities force companies to change tactics

Sticking to the old ways may spell your demise

There is no doubt that going into fiscal 2014, the market will be different. Sequestration and continuing resolutions will take their toll on the federal budget, resulting in fewer procurements. The net result is that competition for the remaining government dollars will be stiffer as companies battle for market share.

Companies that don't change their tactics to compete in the new budget-constrained government market will give way to others who are adapting to these new challenges.

As part of our webinar series on Winning Business in the Government Market, we polled over 300 companies to see what they were doing to raise their competitiveness in the coming year and found some interesting results. Here's what we learned.

How good is your capture process?

The centerpiece of a company's business acquisition campaign is its capture management process. As federal markets shrink, those firms with a defined, repeatable, and well-managed capture process will generally compete better than those who don't have this process in place.

In surveying companies, we found that 22% of the companies have a defined, repeatable, and well-managed capture and proposal process that consistently produces wins. The vast majority of companies surveyed (72%) said they understood capture, but were performing ad hoc without gaining the benefits of a well-defined, repeatable capture process, and 6% of the companies said they had no capture process.

Of the companies we surveyed, 33% said they were managing capture and proposal activities at the enterprise level where they collected information on all company pursuits. Most companies (59%) said they shared some capture and proposal data using shared directories on a server, but without the benefit of a formal enterprise management system for business acquisition.

A few companies (8%) still archive their capture and proposal information on individual PCs and are operating without sharing data.

How good is your competitive pricing?

I was surprised to learn that 28% of the companies surveyed said they had a mature competitive assessment (CA) and price to win (PTW) practice that consistently produced good results. I thought it would have been less.

Sixty-one percent of the companies said that sometimes they did a CA and PTW analysis, but would not characterize the work as having been done consistently or done well.

Finally, 11% of the firms do pricing the old way — they start the night before the proposal is due and work all night to finish just in time to make the delivery.

What's your plan for 2014?

In our final survey question, we postulated that everyone would enter 2014 with a plan to raise their competitiveness given the more challenging market. Assuming this was the case, we asked where firms were placing their emphasis to raise their competitiveness. Almost half (49%) said they would put their emphasis on establishing a capture and proposal process and would include capture analytics as part of that undertaking.

The rest of the companies split the emphasis between improving pricing (24%) and improving the quality of their proposals (22%). As always, some companies just don't have a plan, and in our survey 5% of the firms fell into that category.

An assessment of the competitive landscape

As companies enter a fiercely competitive market, you can sum up the statistics this way.

About 20% of the companies really have their act together and have established an integrated capture and proposal process, have an established analytics program to measure the effectiveness of their capture and proposal processes, and have a well-developed CA and PTW process. They are managing business acquisition as an enterprise rather than as a federation of independent business units. These are the companies that will continue to prosper in the new government market.

Two thirds of the companies are in the middle ground where they have a capture and proposal process and they occasionally do CA and PTW, but all of these companies admit that their processes aren't that good and they need to be improved.

This is really an interesting comment because we know from past experience that many of these companies will argue that they are far too busy doing things poorly to stop and fix their broken processes. Clearly, many of these companies will be in the same situation next year.

Then there is the final 10%. These are the ones that just don't get it. They will always finish at the back of the pack.

In this new level of competitiveness, they will be the first casualties of battle.

WashingtonTechnology.com, September 20, 2013

How crazy subcontractors can kill your bid

Have you ever had a subcontractor kill your bid? Surprisingly, it's not all that infrequent that a subcontractor can do you in.

Here are some of the situations we have seen this year from companies who have called us for help, generally after it is too late to fix the problem. Since many of these teaming nightmares could have been prevented with some good counseling earlier in the bidding process, I thought I would share some of these with you and also offer advice that you can use to keep these problems from happening to you.

Subcontractor teaming restrictions

A recent government solicitation stated that prime contractors were encouraged to team with multiple smaller businesses in order to fulfill the socioeconomic goals of the procurement. The request for proposals further stated that *subcontractors shall be limited to teaming with only one prime contractor and cannot be a subcontractor on multiple teams.* I'm sure you have seen this kind of restricted teaming language before.

The prime contractor who called said they selected their small business subcontractors and executed teaming agreements with each, wrote a fine proposal that was submitted on time, and then got a letter back from the government saying their proposal had been rejected.

They explained that apparently, their subcontractor thought that if teaming with one prime contractor was good, teaming with multiple primes was better. Even though the subcontractor signed an exclusive teaming agreement with the prime contractor, they teamed with multiple companies in order to increase their chances of winning. All prime contractors who teamed with this subcontractor had their proposals rejected.

We told the prime that in the future, when an RFP contains specific language restricting subcontractor teaming, we recommend that this language be included in an addendum to the teaming agreement and the addendum be signed by an executive of the subcontractor certifying that they have teamed in accordance with the teaming restrictions.

Regrettably, in this case, it was too late to correct the problem.

Subcontractor conflict of interest

A solicitation required the prime and its subcontractors to individually certify that they had no organizational conflict of interest (OCI). Less than one week prior to submission, the subcontractor's contracting officer on a related contract indicated he thought the subcontractor had an OCI on the job the company was bidding.

The subcontractor communicated the news to the prime and indicated the issue was resolved. The subcontractor signed the OCI certification, and the prime contractor submitted the proposal. Shortly after the proposal was submitted, the contracting office notified the prime contractor that their bid had been rejected due to the subcontractor's OCI.

The prime contractor challenged the rejection by asking the CO to evaluate the bid without the subcontractor's input, and while the CO sympathized with the prime contractor, the decision rejecting the bid stood.

Clearly, this subcontractor wanted to run from its OCI problem, and signing a statement that a conflict doesn't exist does not make the conflict go away. We advised that the prime get an OCI determination directly from the government before submitting its proposal and if this could not be resolved prior to submission, the prime should either submit an OCI mitigation plan with its proposal or submit an alternate proposal without the subcontractor rather than risk its entire proposal being rejected because of an unresolved OCI problem.

Getting the subcontractor to certify that an OCI problem does not exists is not sufficient since it is the government who is the final arbitrator of whether or not there is an OCI issue. Relying on the subcontractor's certification statement cost the prime contractor its bid.

Subcontractor poor past performance

A prime contractor identified several small businesses that had direct contract experience with the customer and invited these companies to join their team. The sales reps from the small businesses boasted how well they knew the customer, how strong their relationships were, and how insightful they were about the work being competed. It was a perfect match, and the prime signed up the subcontractors.

The prime and the subcontractors worked hard on the proposal. The prime submitted the bid and shortly thereafter was told they lost. In the debriefing, the government indicated the subcontractors' past performance was marginal and was overstated in the proposal. As a result, the government down-scored the proposal based on the poor subcontractor past performance and overstated claims.

I suppose no sales rep has ever told a prime contractor that his/her firm's performance was marginal and they had a lousy relationship with the customer. After all, sales reps wouldn't last very long in that position if they didn't put a positive spin on a marginal situation.

This problem occurs continually in teaming and runs the gamut from stretching the truth to outright lying. Knowing that this goes on, we always recommend that you do your own due diligence. You can trust, but you must always verify and never let a subcontractor's unchecked claims about its past performance sink your proposal.

Subcontractors with extreme incumbentitis

The government changed the size standard on the recompete of a contract, forcing the incumbent to look for a company with the right size standard and socio-economic certification to prime their contract. After careful deliberation, they identified a partner who had a long-term history with the client and an outstanding reputation. The teaming agreement was signed and the proposal was begun.

Next, the incumbent proceeded to make the new prime's life miserable. They developed an extreme case of incumbentitis, could not understand the necessity of improving their processes on the new contract, thought every benefit rested on the argument that they were the incumbent, and were extremely cautious sharing information with the prime contractor even to the detriment of the bid.

The incumbent insisted that the proposal only had to conform with section C (statement of work) of the RFP, not section L (proposal instructions) and section M (proposal evaluation criteria). According to the subcontractor, they never paid attention to L and M, only the SOW. They were quite adamant and disrupted all review meetings.

To resolve these issues, we arbitrated a meeting between the top executives of both firms, resulting in the subcontractor changing out the people supporting the proposal. With new, more-reasonable players involved, progress is being made towards a winning proposal, but much valuable time has been lost in the exercise of forming a highly functioning team. We'll have to wait to see how this one turns out.

A positive outlook on teaming

Not all teaming arrangements turn out badly. If you want to read more about teaming and the characteristics that make teaming successful, refer to *Washington Technology's WT Insider Reports* (http://goo.gl/7w5pgS).

WashingtonTechnology.com, November 18, 2013

How to balance your growth strategy

When I review new-business growth strategies for companies, one of the things I like to see is a balanced approach that consists of three main strategies—winning new business, growing your current business base, and if the company is large enough, acquiring other companies.

As a first cut, I weight each of these strategies equally, so if the company uses all three, then each strategy is accountable for delivering a third of the company's revenue growth. In this case, winning new business would be accountable for delivering a third of the company's growth.

There are important tactics within each of these strategies that need to be present for them to execute well. In this article, I'll discuss some of the tactics that you should look for and how to build your own new-business growth strategy.

Winning new business

The government uses multiple procurement
approaches to award contracts, and every
government contractor should have a new-
business acquisition strategy that aligns with each
of these approaches. If you are planning your
company's business growth strategy, make sure
that your approach includes these four tactics at a
minimum.

General Services Administration schedules

If you are in the IT or professional services
business, you will want to make sure your
company has a General Services Administration
(GSA) IT Schedule 70 contract, a Mission Oriented
Business Integrated Services (MOBIS) contract,
and a Professional Engineering Services (PES)
contract. The government pushed $38 billion
through all of the GSA schedule contracts in fiscal
year 2011 and about the same amount in 2012. Of
that spending, $23 billion (over 60% of all dollars
awarded through GSA schedule buys) went
through these three schedules with the IT

Schedule 70 garnering $15 billion (40% of the total GSA schedule spending).

These three GSA schedules are essential vehicles for closing small and mid-sized new business deals with most government agencies.

Agencies also use these GSA vehicles as the basis for entering into blanket purchase agreements (BPAs), which can put your company in a preferential position to provide products and services to a government agency. Some state and local government organizations also buy off GSA schedules.

To be a leader in the new business game, make sure GSA schedules are part of your growth strategy. If your firm is not a GSA schedule contract holder, then you may find yourself sitting on the sidelines, unable to compete and watching other companies take your business away.

Multiple award contracts

The government often awards contracts to multiple companies for a broad range of services and products and then competes work under these contracts at the task order level.

When these contracts are available to multiple agencies, they are called government wide acquisition contracts (GWACs), and when they are open to just the issuing agency, they are called specific-agency multiple award contracts (MACs).

Additionally, there is another category of contracts called indefinite delivery/indefinite quantity (IDIQ) contracts that may be awarded to a single company or multiple companies.

In all, there are about 600 GWACs, MACs, and IDIQ contracts.

Some of the more popular GWACs are GSA's Alliant contract, the National Institutes of Health's (NIH) Chief Information Officers Solutions and Partners (CIO-SP3), the Defense Information Systems Agency (DISA) Encore II contract, the Office of Personnel Management's (OPM) Training and Management Assistance (TMA) contract, the Army's Information Technology Enterprise Solutions Services (ITES-2S), and many others.

Some multiple award contracts are awarded to just a few companies and others, like the Navy's SeaPort-e contract, has been awarded to 2,400 companies.

As you build out your growth strategy for each government agency, your market research team should determine which multiple award vehicles are most popular as indicated by the dollar value of task orders flowing through each vehicle by agency.

This will give you a clear focus on which multiple award contracts need to be in your portfolio to accelerate your revenue growth with each agency. It is best to have multiple vehicles that can service your target agencies since the popularity of individual vehicles tends to ebb and flow.

Set-aside procurements

Agencies set aside procurements for small business and can limit competition for these contracts to firms that meet the small business size standards set by the Small Business Administration. They can further restrict competitions to firms that are 8(a) certified,

Service Disabled Veteran Owned Small Businesses (SDVOSB), or businesses resident in Historically Underutilized Business (HUB) Zones.

If your firm qualifies for these set-aside procurements, then using these preferential programs will be a main thrust for your business growth strategy.

If you are not eligible to participate in these set-aside procurements as a prime contractor, then you need to have a strategy in place to partner with other firms that can. Again, have your market research team identify those small businesses that have a presence at the agencies you are targeting, and develop relationships with these firms so you are still in the game if a particular agency decides to take the set-aside route for their next procurement.

Full-and-open competitions

These procurements are available to any bidder and are pretty easy to identify on the procurement horizon. Since these are generally the larger-value procurements, they will attract a lot of attention, and competition will be keen. Serious bidders will identify and work these opportunities well in advance with effective capture campaigns and will write highly competitive proposals.

To be successful with the full-and-open growth strategy, you must have the skills and experience to compete in the major league of federal procurements. If you don't have these resources in-house, you will need to augment your staff with professionals who specialize in capture and proposal development for these kinds of procurements.

Grow your current business base

Every member of your company's technical and operational management team should know and understand they have an important role in growing your company's business.

These individuals have a privileged role in BD because they interact with your customers and probably know more about what your customers need than anyone else in your firm. They have the high ground in the campaign for new business.

They can find out information that outsiders can't get, and they can see firsthand what problems your customers have and what services your firm might offer to your customer base. What is missing in most companies is a plan to mobilize these resources.

To grow your current business base, these individuals must be part of your growth campaign. Some fundamental actions include:

- Ensuring these people understand that growing your company's business is part of their role in the company

- Providing appropriate training or coaching in BD, capture management, and proposal writing

- Using a management mechanism to collect and act on the information they provide

- Implementing a mechanism to recognize and reward individuals for successful accomplishment

If you mobilize your operations team, they can accelerate your revenue growth and lead the firm in acquiring new business.

Buying other companies

Acquisitions are generally done to strengthen your company's presence in a market that you are already in or to give your company an operational base in a market that your firm wants to enter for strategic reasons.

If you are planning on making acquisitions part of your growth strategy, then decide what you want to buy (more revenue in your current markets or a strategic position in new markets) and how much you are willing to spend—then get professional assistance in this highly specialized area.

Balancing the strategies

All three growth strategies work well for government contractors.

If you decide you are not ready for acquisitions, then focus your growth strategy in equal amounts on winning new business and growing your current business base.

Some good market research will go a long way in helping you decide which government agencies to target and what services and products to push.

To be effective, you should have a balanced growth strategy, so get going and put this approach to work for your firm.

WashingtonTechnology.com, December 13, 2013

Contractors reshape growth strategies for 2014

Before this past year fades from memory, I thought it would be instructive to take a look back at 2013 and examine how well, or not well, government contractors did in terms of revenue growth and see what companies are doing to reshape their growth strategies for 2014.

To get a handle on the details, Lohfeld Consulting Group joined with Market Connections to jointly poll 220 government contractors to learn how their sales turned out in calendar year 2013 and what changes they were making going forward. Here's what we found out.

15% see positive growth

If your firm's revenue grew at all in 2013, you should feel pretty good because you were an exception in the market. What really surprised us was that only 15% of all companies surveyed reported positive sales growth in 2013. Sixteen percent said revenues were flat, and a whopping 61% reported a downturn in revenues. Eight percent of respondents did not comment on their companies' sales.

Large businesses were more resilient to sales declines than small businesses. Twenty-one percent of the large businesses reported that their revenue declined 10% or more. Thirty-nine percent of small businesses without socioeconomic preferences such as 8(a) firms, Service Disabled Veteran Owned Small Businesses (SDVOSB), Woman Owned Small Businesses (WOSB), and Historically Underutilized Businesses (HUB) Zone reported similar declines. Forty-five percent of small businesses with socioeconomic preferences reported declines of 10% or more. Flat sales were reported by 23% of the large businesses, whereas only 8% of small businesses were able to hold their own with sales flat.

In effect, the budget delays, budget cuts, sequestration, government shutdown, and non-stop uncertainty in the government market absolutely hammered small businesses.

Searching for new markets

Expanding into new markets is the government contractor's battle cry for 2014. Forty-five percent of companies surveyed reported that they are expanding sales into new markets, and 40% are expanding into new government agencies.

More than half (57%) of large businesses surveyed are moving into international markets, whereas only 19% of small businesses are adopting an international growth strategy.

The figures are reversed when it comes to expanding into state and local government markets. Fifty-eight percent of small businesses are moving into state, local, and municipal markets, whereas only 36% of large businesses are moving in this direction. Similarly, 23% of small businesses are moving to sell to associations and non-profits, whereas only 7% of large businesses are targeting this market sector as a growth strategy.

Forty percent of companies are expanding sales into new federal agencies. The most popular expansion markets are energy, health services, veteran affairs, public safety, law enforcement, transportation, and finance.

This focus on new government markets is not unexpected since a well-established growth strategy is to expand sales with current customers and move into adjacent markets.

Improving competitiveness

While searching for new markets is important, we also found that contractors are working to improve their acquisition of new business, including reworking processes, adding tools, and moving to agile staffing strategies in order to better match resources to workloads. On the operations side, companies are restructuring organizations to better align with their revised market strategies and moving to reduce internal costs to gain competitive pricing advantages. Some of these initiatives are highlighted below.

Improving capture and proposal processes

This was one of the strongest trends we saw in the survey. Forty-five percent of large companies said they are working on improving their capture and proposal processes, and 34% of small businesses were doing the same thing.

This trend is reinforced by survey data that showed 30% of large businesses and 25% of small businesses are making investments in capture and proposal tools and enterprise infrastructure.

Clearly, the competitive game has moved to the left on the business acquisition timeline, and companies are working to improve business acquisition processes, investing in tools, and building infrastructure to support these new processes.

Outsourcing more services

There is a strong trend toward outsourcing services rather than staffing up internally to provide this capability. Companies are reshaping organizations and resources to better match market dynamics. This is particularly true in capture, proposal development, market research, and recruiting.

Only 12% of companies said they are hiring personnel to write proposals, and just 7% said they are hiring market researchers. We believe these low numbers indicate that most companies are using an agile staffing strategy where they contract for these skills on an as-needed basis rather than staff up internally to provide these services.

Adding business development resources

Thirty-nine percent of the companies surveyed said they were adding BD personnel. This was especially true for the larger businesses. Forty-three percent of large firms reported that they were adding these skills in contrast to 32% of small businesses.

Most likely, companies are adding these skills to address new or adjacent markets as part of their quest to seek out new revenue sources.

Realigning organizations

Several companies reported consolidating business units as they strive to better align resources with new market strategies. For some companies, their organizational realignment

included adding solution developers or support
staff to business groups.

Training

Companies are also stepping up their training in
BD, capture, and proposal development. We find
this a solid strategy since well-trained business
acquisition teams will always return dividends to
the company.

Reducing costs

We also saw cost cutting as a major initiative.
Reducing indirect costs throughout the
organization seems to be a consistent objective in
large and small businesses. Operations are being
reviewed to reduce fixed and variable costs
wherever practical.

Other companies indicated they are outsourcing
services as part of their cost-cutting strategy,
especially when workloads—such as proposal
management and proposal writing—tend to
fluctuate significantly.

Moving forward in 2014

Now is a good time to assess your company's overall strategy for 2014, particularly if your firm was one of the many contractors who had flat or negative sales in 2013. If you choose to continue to do the same things you did in 2013 and expect results to improve in 2014, you will likely be disappointed.

Companies are changing the way they compete, and updating your growth strategy and improving your competitiveness should be among your major initiatives for 2014.

WashingtonTechnology.com, January 15, 2014

What makes your bid a winner or a loser?

I was asked to review a major best-value bid for a firm that was notified they had lost and wanted to protest.

Emotions were running high, and they were making all sorts of allegations about the government not wanting them to win. I asked to see their debriefing file, and what I discovered was surprising—at least to me.

Like many companies, they failed to understand why companies lose and what it takes to win.

Why do you write proposals?

Always remember that proposals are written for one purpose—to convey the information the government evaluators need to select your company over others in the competition.

Proposals are not written to show the government how smart you are or to brag about your company history. They are not written to showcase your

team members or to boast about your world-class
best practices.

Proposals are written to score *points* with the evaluators

When evaluators tally your *points*, they are
generally not talking about a numerical score, but
instead the number of strengths and weaknesses
they give your proposal when they read and score
it.

The real purpose of your proposal is to convey
your strengths to the evaluation team and show
that your offer has no weaknesses.

Strengths are features in your proposal that either
increase the likelihood of successful contract
performance or offer to exceed a contract
requirement in a way that is beneficial to the
government. Some RFPs define additional
characteristics for strengths, but in general, this is
a pretty good definition for a proposal evaluation
strength.

For features to be scored as strengths, they need to
be unique to your proposal or unique to several

proposals because if every bidder proposes the same feature, then that feature will not be scored as a strength.

Your job as a capture manager and/or proposal manager is to ensure your proposal is rich in strengths and that each of your strengths gets conveyed clearly to the evaluation committee, who will in turn brief those strengths to the source selection official.

To have a winning proposal, you must do more than just respond to the proposal instructions and evaluation criteria. Your proposal must be compelling—rich in strengths—and have no weaknesses.

Picking the losers

I have always maintained that the government picks losers first, and the last bidder left standing is the winner in the source selection process. Here's how it works.

The proposal evaluation team briefs the SSO on the strengths, weaknesses, deficiencies, and price of each offer. Some agencies include significant strengths and significant weaknesses in the briefing. With this information, the SSO performs an independent determination of which offer represents the best value to the government and documents these findings in the contract file.

In practice, the SSO eliminates offers from further consideration based on their deficiencies, weaknesses, lack of strengths, and price. If your bid has one or more deficiencies, it is game over. Your bid is set aside as a loser, and you lost in the SSO's first evaluation pass.

If your proposal has no deficiencies, but has multiple weaknesses not offset by multiple strengths, you will be in the next round of losers selected. If your proposal has no deficiencies or weaknesses, but has fewer strengths compared to other bidders, you will be next in line as a loser.

If your price is too high, you will be moved to the next group of losers. After all, there is a price above which the government will not pay no matter how good your proposal is.

This process of selecting losers continues until only a few bidders are left in the race. At this point, the SSO may look beyond the number of strengths. The SSO examines the merit of each strength, and compares the value of these strengths and your bid price with other finalists.

Bidders continue to be deselected until just one bidder remains. In the final analysis, the last bidder left standing is the winner.

Disgruntled bidder

The proposal that I reviewed was clearly a loser in spite of being well written and having no deficiencies. As we would say in the trade of writing professional proposals, it was compliant and responsive.

What it lacked was a compelling technical approach. The disgruntled bidder scored only two strengths in their technical approach, while other bidders scored eight to ten strengths in the same sections.

I told the disgruntled bidder they failed to engineer evaluation strengths into their technical approach, and that is what cost them the win.

Best Informed Wins

Volume 2 – Collected Articles of Bob Lohfeld
from *Washington Technology* (2013 – 2015)

A sound technical approach with no weaknesses is necessary, but not sufficient to win. They now understand that they have to outscore their competitors, and in the end, it is all about evaluation strengths.

WashingtonTechnology.com, February 14, 2014

Six tips for building your new business pipeline

Most companies really miss the mark when building their new business pipeline

Typically, the market research team dumps every conceivable deal they can find into the new business pipeline. One company that I reviewed even boasted that they had a new business pipeline with over 150 targets worth $8 billion. With a win probability of 5%, they thought they could bring in $400 million in new sales.

Their new business pipeline was nothing more than a pipedream. Let's get real and follow these six simple tips when building a new business pipeline.

Stay close to your core business

A fundamental truth in BD is that the better you understand the customer, the more likely you are to win. Always apply this principle when building your new business pipeline, and start by looking for new business opportunities with your current customers or with organizations that are close to your current customers.

Look at your current customers' organization charts and see what adjacent organizations do and what they are buying. If they are buying similar services, then these procurements should be high-priority deals in your new business pipeline.

Don't overlook opportunities to be a subcontractor if the kinds of services you are providing are being bundled into larger competitive procurements. Additionally, look for procurement opportunities to support your customer in other geographic locations. It's often easy to identify opportunities where your customer is buying the same services that you are providing currently—except the procurements cover other geographic locations.

Don't hesitate to ask for referrals from your current customers. If you are doing an excellent job, your customers will want to refer you to others.

Look at what else your current customer is buying

It is often easier to sell new services to your current customers than to sell those services to new customers. Always look at what else your current customers are buying.

If your firm is a service provider, you may have broad capabilities to support a current customer who may be unaware that your firm could provide additional services. Perhaps you are only getting a small percentage of what your customer is buying today, and it may be easy to convince your customer to buy from you rather than from another contractor.

Look at what else your customers are buying and ask the question, could your firm provide these services too? If so, add these opportunities to your new business pipeline.

Set a strategy for targeting new agencies

When you select opportunities in new agencies, make sure you have a rationale for why you want to prospect in those agencies, and make sure that the work closely matches the scope of your current or past work. If you are in the health care business, it makes sense for you to prospect for work in other agencies that do health care work.

On the other hand, if the agency is not in the health care business, and that is what your firm does, selling to them will be more difficult.

Have a strategy that reinforces the business that you are in or want to be in and then look for opportunities in agencies that fit your strategy. If you're a service provider, don't let your market research team search across the entire government landscape to pick opportunities. If you do, you will discover you are prospecting in 50 different agencies, and you'll learn it is very difficult to convert your new business opportunities into revenue.

Trying to be a credible bidder in too many agencies generally turns out to be a useless waste of time and energy.

If you are selling hardware or software licenses, then you can select more agencies. With commodity offerings, you can be a mile wide and an inch deep in the government market and have a successful strategy.

Avoid chasing the gold rush

Everyone wants to be where the action is, but before you go chasing new agencies and leaping into new lines of business, make sure you are going to be successful.

It is easy to see that every IT company wants to be in cybersecurity, but if you have no company past performance, experience, tools, or technical staff in this market, then maybe it is better to avoid racing in where others have more compelling credentials.

Selling new services that you haven't sold before to customers that have not bought from you previously is nearly impossible in a crowded government market. While it is tempting to have the market research team follow the money, it can often land you in places where you are just an outsider watching others take the business away.

Focus is key

There are always going to be targeted opportunities that pop up along your journey, and these will deserve your full attention, but for the most part, focusing your new business pipeline on agencies where you have traction or can reasonably hope to get traction is a good idea.

The scope of your market coverage will depend on the size of your firm. The smaller the firm, the tighter your focus should be. Larger firms are less concerned about focus and more concerned about deal size. After all, these companies didn't get to be king of the jungle by chasing rabbits.

Stay focused and be reasonable with the scope of your new business pipeline. There is no point in building into your pipeline more agencies or deals than you have the resources to explore.

Developing relationships with government executives

I believe it is equally as important to focus on developing relationships with government executives as it is to chase deals.

The reason is that many of the deals are not visible to an outside market researcher and can only be discovered or created through face-to-face discussions with potential users of your services or products.

I've often called this the *Lewis and Clark* strategy in honor of the two explorers who set out to find a safe route to the Pacific Northwest. It took them over 2 years to reach the Pacific Ocean, but the things they learned along the way were just as valuable as the destination. It's the same in BD. It's the people you meet and the opportunities you discover along the way that will pay off for you even if you never bid the big deal that you started out chasing.

When developing your new business pipeline, identify all the people you need to meet along the way, and see if you can discover what they need. These exploratory discussions will identify opportunities that are never publicized. They are the ones your market research team will never see from their 30,000-foot view, but you can discover them when you focus your discussions with the government executives you meet along the way.

How effective is your new business pipeline?

Over time, you can measure the effectiveness of your new business pipeline and your market research efforts. Some companies learn that very few, if any, of their new business wins came from the targets they identified from their market research efforts. In these cases, some corrective actions need to occur.

Hopefully, following these tips will help turn last year's pipedream into this year's new business pipeline.

WashingtonTechnology.com, March 19, 2014

How good are your chances of winning a bid protest?

Your chance of winning a protest may be better than you think, but that depends on how you define winning.

Last year, the Government Accountability Office (GAO) decided only 3.43% of its protests cases in favor of the protester, but that is only part of the story.

In a large number of protests, the procuring agency took voluntary corrective action granting some form of relief to the protester, thereby preempting GAO from rendering a protest decision. When adding these cases to those GAO decided in favor of the protester, the effectiveness rate for protests soars to 43%. In this article, we will take a closer look at what this means for bidders and what they might expect from protests.

Protest sustainment rate

In GAO's 2013 annual report to Congress on bid
protests (http://goo.gl/ip50Oa), GAO reported that
it sustained bidder protests for 87 protest cases out
of 2,538 cases it closed that year. This is a protest
win rate of 3.43% for all protest cases closed. Of
the 2,538 cases closed, 259 cases, or about 10%,
were attributable to GAO's bid protest jurisdiction
over task orders or delivery orders placed under
indefinite delivery/indefinite quantity (IDIQ)
contracts.

The most prevalent reasons for sustaining protests
in 2013 were:

- Failure of the procuring agency to follow
  the solicitation evaluation criteria

- Inadequate documentation of the record

- Unequal treatment of offerors

- Unreasonable price or cost evaluation

- Voluntary corrective actions

In over 1,000 bid protest cases last year, the procuring agencies voluntarily took corrective actions granting some form of relief to the protester rather than defend the protest on the merits of the case. Corrective action can occur at any time during a protest.

An agency's corrective action may involve a re-evaluation of proposals, a new award decision, an amendment to a solicitation, or other actions. Typically, GAO dismisses a protest if an agency takes corrective action that resolves protest arguments or provides the relief sought by the protester.

If you filed a protest in 2013, you had a 39.5% chance that the procuring agency would take voluntary corrective action that would result in some form of relief for the protester. When the number of cases where the agency voluntarily took corrective action is added to the number of cases decided in favor of the protester, the effectiveness rate for protesters rises to 43%.

Best Informed Wins

Volume 2 – Collected Articles of Bob Lohfeld
from *Washington Technology* (2013 – 2015)

Protest effectiveness rate

The protest effectiveness rate (protests sustained plus voluntary corrective actions divided by total of all protest cases closed) has been pretty constant over the past 5 years, ranging from a low of 42% to a high of 45%.

Similarly, the sustainment rate for protests (protests sustained divided by total number of protests sustained and denied) has largely held constant, ranging from a low of 16% to a 19% high.

While these rates have remained fairly constant, the number of protests brought each year has generally increased. From 2009 to 2013, the number of protests filed increased from 1,989 to 2,429 or an increase of about 22%. The number of protests filed each year from 2009 increased every year with the exception of 2013, when the number of protests declined from 2012 by about 2%.

This decline is presumably due to reduced government spending and reduced number of procurement actions in 2013.

Not all protests go the distance. Only about 20% of GAO protests are actually decided on the merit of the protest, so there is a four out of five chance that the protest will be dismissed by GAO because the protest had a technical or procedural flaw (such as lack of timeliness or jurisdiction), the agency took corrective action that addressed the protest, or the protester withdrew the protest because it decided it could not win.

Your best protest outcomes

If you are planning to protest, probably the best outcome would be for the agency to voluntarily take corrective action quickly so GAO could dismiss the protest early in the process, saving you some legal expenses. Your chance of this happening is around 40%.

If the protest goes the distance, your chance of winning drops to less than 20%.

So if the agency doesn't voluntarily take corrective action, you might want to consider pulling the plug on your protest and saving the little bit of money you have left to bid other jobs where you have a better chance of winning.

WashingtonTechnology.com, April 28, 2014

How and when to talk to your customer

Bob Lohfeld tracks the misconceptions about communications during the procurement process

Everyone seems to want better communication between government and industry during the procurement process, and yet when we ask how well government and industry communicate, the answer is always the same—not very well.

One reasonably knowledgeable procurement official explained to me that the reason for this is that if he talks with one company, then he has to talk with all of them, and he simply doesn't have time to do that. Instead, he makes it his practice to talk with no one. Wow! We all want a level playing field when it comes to federal procurement, but nowhere do the rules say the government has to level every player.

How could this procurement official have gotten it so wrong? Here's some insight into what the rules are for communication during the acquisition life cycle.

Review Federal Acquisition Regulation rules

From the government's point of view, the earliest communication with industry is considered market research, and the regulations for doing that are found in Federal Acquisition Regulation (FAR) Part 10 (http://goo.gl/47rVlo). Market research is necessary to arrive at the most suitable approach for acquiring supplies and services. Agencies must conduct market research appropriate to the circumstances of the acquisition before developing new requirements documents and before awarding a task or delivery order under an indefinite delivery/indefinite quantity (IDIQ) contract. The extent of market research can vary, depending on such factors as urgency, estimated dollar value, complexity, and past experience.

The techniques for conducting market research are set out in FAR 10.2 and may include any or all of the following:

- Contacting knowledgeable individuals in government and industry regarding market capabilities to meet requirements

- Publishing formal Requests for Information (RFI) in appropriate technical or scientific journals or business publications

- Participating in interactive, on-line communication among industry, acquisition personnel, and customers

- Conducting interchange meetings or holding pre-solicitation conferences to involve potential offerors early in the acquisition process

FAR Part 15 (http://goo.gl/L8954B) sets out the rules for negotiated procurements, and FAR 15.2 specifically addresses communicating with industry before receipt of proposals. It states that exchanges of information among all interested parties are encouraged from the earliest identification of a requirement through receipt of proposals.

The purpose of exchanging information is to improve the understanding of government requirements and industry capabilities, thereby allowing potential offerors to judge whether or how they can satisfy the government's requirements; enhancing the government's ability to obtain quality supplies and services, including construction, at reasonable prices; and increasing efficiency in proposal preparation, proposal evaluation, negotiation, and contract award.

Early exchange of information among industry and the program manager, contracting officer, and other acquisition process participants can identify and resolve concerns regarding:

- Acquisition strategy, including proposed contract type, terms and conditions, and acquisition planning schedules

- Feasibility of the requirement, including performance requirements, statements of work, and data requirements

- Suitability of the proposal instructions and evaluation criteria, including the approach for assessing past performance information

- Availability of reference documents

- Any other industry concerns or questions

The only caveat about these communications is that when specific information necessary for preparation of proposals is disclosed to one or more potential offerors, that information must be made available to the public as soon as practicable, but no later than the next general release of information, to avoid creating an unfair competitive advantage.

Best practices in government

Much has been written about government best practices in communicating with industry, and yet we still see misinterpretations of the rules.

The latest guidance that I have read is from Air Force Col. Michael Claffey, deputy director of contracting at the Air Force Life Cycle Management Center at Hanscom Air Force Base. In his memorandum, *Golden Rules for*

Communication and Early Industry Involvement (http://goo.gl/5tJ0c1), Claffey stresses that industry should be informed of upcoming acquisitions as soon as the needs have been identified.

Initiating early contact with industry allows time for industry feedback, which helps the government develop realistic requirements. By giving contractors more time to prepare for an acquisition, they will be able to provide better solutions for the government.

The most comprehensive guidance has come from Dan Gordon, former administrator of Federal Procurement Policy, in his Myth Busting memorandum, *Addressing the Misconceptions to Improve Communication with Industry During the Acquisition Process* (http://goo.gl/xmJZFD).

In this Myth Busting memo, he takes on the misconception about government meeting one-on-one with potential offers. His guidance is clear—the government can generally meet one-on-one with potential offerors as long as no vendor receives preferential treatment.

"Prior to issuance of a solicitation, government officials—including the program manager, users or contracting officer—may meet with potential offerors to exchange general information and conduct market research related to an acquisition. There is no requirement that meetings include all possible offerors, nor is there a prohibition against one-on-one meetings," Gordon wrote.

Best practices in industry

There is equally good guidance offered for industry when it comes to communicating with government. In her Myth Busting–2 memorandum, *Addressing the Misconceptions and Further Improving Communication with Industry During the Acquisition Process* (http://goo.gl/pXQ9xJ), Lesley Field, also a former administrator of Federal Procurement Policy, offers good guidance addressing industry's misconceptions about communicating with government.

For example, some industry executives are concerned that if they meet one-on-one with agency personnel, these personnel may share their proprietary information with other competitors;

yet agency personnel have an obligation to protect proprietary information from disclosure outside the government or to other competitors.

Similarly, Myth Busting–2 deals with the misconception that the best way to present your company's capabilities is by marketing directly to the CO and/or signing them up on your company mailing list. It points out that COs and program managers are often inundated with general marketing information that doesn't reach the right people at the right time, making this method often ineffective.

Making communications meaningful

When I talk with government executives about what industry can do to improve communications, there is a consistent, recurring theme that we need to make communications more meaningful and relevant. Gone are the days when a government program manager wanted to listen to a generic capability presentation where your firm briefed 47 competency areas just to see if the government wanted to buy any of it. There is a forum for briefing capabilities, but it is not in a one-on-one meeting with a government program manager.

Program managers are interested in how you can help them solve their problem or provide services better, faster, or cheaper. To have meaningful, relevant communications, you need to do your research before the meeting, come in well prepared knowing what you want to learn and what you want to share, and most of all, provide information that is relevant to the government program manager's mission. If you do this, you can have a productive, meaningful exchange of information.

As one CIO explained, if you are 5 minutes into your briefing and you are still explaining your company's org chart, the meeting is pretty much over, and the only person in the room who doesn't know it is the person doing the briefing.

Be prepared and be focused, and then the government will want to hear what you have to say.

WashingtonTechnology.com, June 18, 2014

Take your proposal from good to great in 30 minutes

Thirty minutes is all the time you need to redirect the writing of a mediocre proposal and put it on a clear path to victory. In this article, I'll explain how to use this simple yet effective technique.

Proposal mediocrity

We had just finished a Red Team review on a typical 100-page proposal. The proposal manager instructed the review team on how to do an effective Red Team review. The reviewers had done an excellent job reviewing the proposal and documenting their comments electronically.

They briefed the proposal team, and it was clear what needed to be done. While the proposal team could easily turn the comments in 48 hours and make the repairs needed to the proposal, there was a sense that the proposal just didn't come across as a winner.

The proposal team knew they had done an admirable job building a compliant proposal outline that was easily traceable to the RFP instructions and evaluation criteria. The review team confirmed that the proposal text was, for the most part, compliant with the RFP. They pointed out where additional content was needed and where text and graphics could be improved, and they provided additional content that would help make the proposal more responsive to the requirements.

Yet, the team still had an uneasy feeling that it takes more to win than building a compliant, responsive bid.

We have talked in previous articles about the seven factors we use to build winning proposals; the first two of these factors are compliance and responsiveness. But these alone are not sufficient to win.

A proposal must provide a compelling offer, rich in features that can be scored as strengths, and this is where our proposal was falling short. It was at best, a *ho-hum*, compliant, responsive bid without any distinguishing characteristics that would make it a winner. Enthusiasm lagged as no one had any brilliant ideas as to the path forward.

I'm sure you have seen this situation many times before. The team is demoralized, but still committed to hunker down and go the distance to make this the best proposal they can.

Getting the proposal back on track

I explained to the team that writing a great proposal is often similar to creating a great oil painting. The great masters like Rembrandt and Rubens always created their oil paintings in three distinct layers—the foundation layer, the middle layer, and the final glaze layer.

I explained to the team that like artwork, they had created a foundation layer with a compliant proposal structure. They were midway through completing the middle layer, which is the responsive text that fills in all the voids in the proposal structure, and they were now ready to begin the final layer that provides the highlights and luster that are so recognizable in great art.

In proposals, the winning layer is the features of your offer that the evaluators can score as strengths. You must highlight each strength in the appropriate place in your proposal in order to receive the maximum score. And, of course, you do not want to have any weaknesses.

For government proposals, strengths must meet the *strength test*—features that exceed a contract requirement in a way that is beneficial to the government or increase the likelihood of mission or contract accomplishment. These strengths must be unique to your offer, or at least not offered by all bidders. Strengths are always tied to the evaluation factors or subfactors.

Building the final layer of the proposal

I instructed the proposal team and the reviewers to create an email message addressed to me, the capture manager, and the proposal manager. Next, write four headers in the email—one for each evaluation factor.

In this case, the evaluation factors were Technical Approach, Management Plan, Transition Plan, and Past Performance.

Next, I asked them to simulate writing their own briefing to the source selection official. The briefing had to follow the RFP evaluation factors and include each of the major strengths or significant strengths of the offer tied to the appropriate evaluation factor.

They were not constrained by what was written in the proposal. Instead, I asked them to write down all the reasons (strengths) that their offer should be selected for this award. This heads-down, independent exercise gave them 5 minutes to list all the features they want the SSO to find. They had 5 minutes to write down as many noteworthy strengths as possible cross-walked to the evaluation factors. Everyone was done within the 5-minute timeline.

Next, we did a roll call of each member of the proposal review and writing teams asking them to tell us what strengths they had written for the first evaluation factor. We had 20 people on the call, so in the next 5 minutes, all 20 people debriefed their strengths for the first factor. We then went to the next evaluation factor and continued until all four evaluation factors were briefed.

With the final roll call, the team had identified about 100 features that could potentially be scored as strengths. Yet, 80% of these identified strengths had not made it into the proposal.

This situation is not unusual because the writing process often focuses only on compliance and responsiveness to the RFP instructions. Writers respond to the RFP instructions rather than the strengths that are essential to winning. Many participants identified the same strengths under an evaluation factor. These are likely to be the strengths that the evaluators will find as well.

To wrap up the process, I asked the participants to take an additional 5 minutes to ensure every strength had a well-identified feature with a corresponding benefit offered to the customer and at least one proof point that substantiated the claim. Each strength must include a feature/benefit/proof construct in order to receive a maximum score, so I asked everyone to make sure their email followed that structure.

At the 30-minute mark, I asked everyone to hit the *Send* key, and the exercise was done. I told them the proposal team would review each suggested strength, deliberate whether or not it met the strength test, and then place it in the proposal where each would receive the highest score.

Within 30 minutes, the morale of the proposal and review team had changed. Everyone could see the final layer of the proposal taking shape and bringing the luster and brightness that was promised. The final layer transformed a dull, *ho-hum*, compliant, responsive bid into a winning proposal.

Of course, the proposal team still had more to do in order to polish this bid into a winning proposal. However, the trajectory of the bid had been lifted from a mediocre response to a winning offer in just 30 minutes.

Give it a try and let me know if it works for you.

WashingtonTechnology.com, July 28, 2014

Let's stop bashing LPTA and find an alternative

One of the things I dislike most about lowest priced, technically acceptable (LPTA) procurements is that they are so misaligned with the values we have grown up with as government contractors.

No matter how hard I try, I just cannot get excited about writing a proposal where the objective is to provide the minimally acceptable technical solution—a solution that just squeaks by the technical evaluators—instead of one that dazzles them by striving for outstanding performance and showcases good ideas and innovations. I was brought up in an industry that prided itself on striving to be the best, and not one that sought to deliver minimally acceptable work to the government.

I'm not alone in this belief. In the *2014 Washington Technology Insider Report on LPTA procurements* (http://goo.gl/jNBpjf), 89% of industry and government responded that they were opposed to the use of LPTA for services procurements.

Additionally, this view is shared by Frank Kendall, Under Secretary of Defense for Acquisition, Technology and Logistics, in his directive called *Better Buying Power 2.0* (http://goo.gl/Oc9fuW), which says that LPTA bids are inappropriate for procurements when the government would receive any value from proposals offering to exceed the minimum technical or performance requirements and specifically calls out professional services bids as generally falling into this category.

With such overwhelming opposition to the use of LPTA procurements, you have to wonder why they continue to show up in services bids.

While the government intended LPTA procurements to reduce acquisition costs, we've also seen that LPTA can reduce proposal evaluation periods and avoid protests. Proposal evaluations are being done by first reviewing price proposals to find the lowest priced offeror, and then only that proposal is submitted for technical review.

If evaluators find that proposal to be technically acceptable, the evaluation is done, and the remaining proposals are never evaluated for technical acceptability. Because government awards to the lowest price offeror, there is little to protest other than the technical acceptability of that offeror. The unintended consequence is that LPTA bids are being used to sidestep protests and make awards quickly to the boldest contractor, and not necessarily the best contractor.

If we are going to move away from LPTA bids, then we must offer an alternative that helps the government achieve lower acquisition costs, while not sacrificing performance in the process. We need a bid structure that lets industry strive for excellence, but also share in the government's objective to drive down the cost of service delivery.

If industry and government can share these values, then we will get procurement back on track, and LPTA will become an artifact of commodity procurements—its original intention.

Aligning industry and government values

Two fundamental values—technical and financial—must move into alignment for both government and industry to achieve their respective goals. The technical value is the easiest to align.

Let's all agree that striving for excellence, rather than minimally acceptable performance, is a shared value and that in complex technical and professional services bids, the government always receives additional value when minimum technical and performance standards are exceeded.

Let's continue to evaluate technical and management proposals for their excellence and award evaluation strengths as we have traditionally done in best value tradeoff procurements.

Financial objectives are a little more difficult to align since industry generally strives to increase profits, and government strives to hold down service delivery costs. However, these two values are not mutually exclusive.

Suppose your next RFP included language that required each bidder to propose a Cost Avoidance and Cost Reduction plan as part of its management approach.

The government would hold a cost reduction meeting with the contractor every 6 months to collaborate on ways to reduce service delivery costs. To make this financially meaningful for the contractor, the contractor needs to share financially in the cost reductions. Here's an example of how this might work.

Suppose the government awards a time-and-materials (T&M) contract for IT services, and the contractor staffs the project with a specified number of people to do the work. Normally, the contractor has no incentive to reduce its project staff because any reduction would reduce its revenue and profits.

However, if the government agreed to share 20% of the cost reduction with the contractor, then the contractor's profits would increase significantly for each person removed from the project, and the government's cost would go down by 80% of the cost each person had been billing prior to removal from the project.

Under this arrangement, financial values move into alignment; for each person removed from the project, the government's costs go down and the contractor's profits go up. It's a win-win situation.

Another advantage of this approach is that it moves evaluation of the plan for cost savings into the technical and management proposals where it can be evaluated on its merit and will place emphasis on full lifecycle cost management—not just initial bid prices. This will move awards away from reckless bidders who take a deep dive on bid price, and instead, favor those bidders who offer a more thoughtful and long-term approach to reducing service delivery costs.

For those who say this cannot be done, I want to remind everyone that the most powerful statement in the Federal Acquisition Regulations (FAR) is its guiding principles in FAR 1.102(d) which reads, "The role of each member of the Acquisition Team is to exercise personal initiative and sound business judgment in providing the best value product or service to meet the customer's needs. In exercising initiative, Government members of the acquisition team may assume if a specific strategy, practice, policy or procedure is in the best interest of the Government and is not addressed in the FAR, nor prohibited by law (statute or case law), Executive order, or other regulation, that the strategy, practice, policy, or procedure is a permissible exercise of authority."

In other words, if it is not specifically prohibited, then it is permissible.

Let's stop bashing LPTA and instead, let's turn loose our collective creativity and find a way to replace it with an approach that is a win-win for everyone. I'm sure there are other ideas out there to bring government and industry values into better alignment.

If you have seen such ideas be successful, please share them with me at *RLohfeld@LohfeldConsulting.com.*

WashingtonTechnology.com, September 2, 2014

Should we have procurement reform or just improvement?

It seems like everyone has been jumping on the procurement reform bandwagon this year and has been saying that the government's procurement system is broken. While reforming government procurement is a lofty goal and resonates well in the halls of Congress, the practicality is that it is more of a pre-election battle cry than a reality.

One organization, the Association of Proposal Management Professionals (APMP) (http://www.apmp.org/), has taken a different approach, stating that the Federal Acquisition Regulations (FAR) — the rules that control government procurement — are fine and do not need to be overhauled. What is broken is the way the FAR is applied and interpreted in many government procurements.

According to APMP in their just-released survey report, *Closing the Procurement Execution Gap* (http://goo.gl/ROFYej), most government and industry professionals strongly agree about what improvements need to be made and how they can be done without reforming the FAR. I hope that BD and capture managers will share APMP's findings with government procurement officials and help spread their recommendations about how to conduct better procurements. Here are some of the more interesting findings.

Limiting LPTA to commodity buys

Using lowest priced, technically acceptable (LPTA) evaluation criteria for services bids has been increasing, yet the APMP survey of over 500 professionals in government and industry involved in government procurements does not support this trend.

According to the survey, 81.8% of industry respondents and 71.7% of government respondents recommend limiting LPTA procurements to commodity bids. These results are very similar to those found in *Washington Technology's* own survey, *LPTA: A Hate-Hate Relationship* (http://goo.gl/Vj0f1m). Most industry and government respondents are in strong agreement that LPTA bids should be curtailed to commodities.

Get access early in the procurement process

Serious bidders are always interested in gaining access to the government in the early stages of a procurement to better understand customer needs and help government understand what capabilities exist in industry.

The government refers to this early-stage interaction as market research. The APMP survey asked industry how well this process is working, and the results point out that this is a good area for further improvement.

Only 18.4% of industry respondents said the government almost always responds to their queries and is generally available to meet with representatives from their companies.

Most industry respondents (52.9%) said the situation was more challenging and they can sometimes get meetings, but those meetings are difficult to get. Some said the government generally avoids their requests (14%), does not return emails or phone calls, and does not want to meet with their organizations. Finally, 14.7% said they didn't know if this was working or not.

Keeping communications open with industry

FAR 15.201 states that, "After release of the solicitation, the contracting officer must be the focal point of any exchange with potential offerors." Some procurement officials are moving the communications cutoff date to the left and closing down communications with industry well before RFP release.

Some agencies cut off communications when a draft RFP is released and some even earlier when a Request for Information (RFI) is released. I have even seen one agency close off communications after completing their market research effort and initiate the communications blackout period more than a year before RFP release.

The survey showed that 93.3% of industry and 73.9% of government recommended keeping communications open until final release of the

RFP. Clearly, there is strong agreement that communications between industry and government should remain open until RFP release and not cut off prematurely.

Using RFIs to prequalify bidders

The government uses RFIs as part of their market research to help set technical requirements for future procurements and decide procurement strategies. Some procurements use RFIs to screen potential bidders and then discourage unqualified companies from bidding. The survey asked respondents if they favored using RFIs to prequalify bidders and then have the government create a short list to receive the final RFP.

There was strong agreement among government and industry that this was a good idea—78.4% of industry and 74.4% of government favored using RFIs to prequalify bidders.

Improve effectiveness of industry days

Industry days are events where the government invites bidders to attend a procurement announcement meeting and presents the requirements for a planned procurement. Often, bidders will fly in multiple people for these meetings only to discover that everything the government presented was already in the published RFP.

The result is that industry representatives come away saying they didn't learn anything from the meeting that they didn't already know.

Some agencies use industry days as an opportunity to engage in one-on-one discussions with bidders after the general briefing to industry. This practice has been well received by both government and industry, and the survey confirms this finding with 87% of industry and 73.9% of government agreeing that industry days should include one-on-one meetings with prime bidders.

Proposal instructions needed

Often government releases draft RFPs without including the proposal instructions and evaluation criteria. Industry uses these draft RFPs to make early bid decisions, but without the proposal instructions and evaluation criteria, companies

don't have all the information needed to make
good pursuit and/or bid decisions.

Most companies start writing their proposals upon
draft RFP release, but without proposal
instructions and evaluation criteria, they risk that
whatever they write will not be usable upon final
RFP release.

In the survey, there was moderate agreement
about releasing complete draft RFPs with 86.8% of
industry and 66.7% of government agreeing that
draft RFPs should include proposal instructions
and evaluation criteria. Industry needs to do a
better job of communicating the importance of
having proposal instructions and evaluation
criteria in draft RFPs. If government better
understands the importance of this, we will begin
seeing more complete draft RFPs being released.

Communicate RFP release dates and delays

When RFPs are not released on time, the cost can
be extraordinary to industry. In anticipation of an
RFP release, bidders begin to assemble their team
of managers, subject matter experts, and proposal

writers by pulling them from other assignments in order to be ready when the RFP drops.

When the RFP is not released on schedule, bidders often keep their proposal team in place—especially when a short delay is expected. However, short delays have a way of turning into long delays, and soon each bidder will have spent a small fortune keeping their teams on standby for an imminent RFP release.

In the survey, 95.6% of industry and 69.5% of government agreed that government must do a better job of establishing RFP release dates and then update them when there is a delay.

Respondents recommended that government use a website to update the RFP release date frequently once they issue a draft RFP. From the survey statistics, it is clear that industry feels the pain when RFP release dates drift to the right, but not all government procurement personnel understand the critical importance of having an accurate RFP release date and keeping industry informed of delays.

Reducing the frequency of protests

If government and industry communications improved, there would be fewer protests. The survey confirms this belief, in part, with 50.9% of industry and 20.5% of government respondents believing that there would be fewer protests if the government better communicated requirements and problems with industry proposals.

Since industry files the protests, not government, I'll lean on the industry statistics to substantiate the position that better communications may mean fewer protests. Surprisingly, 61.5% of government respondents and only 26.8% of industry respondents believe that there would be fewer protests if the government put more rigor into their proposal evaluation process and made sure they evaluated each proposal carefully against the stated evaluation criteria.

Only 22.3% of industry and 17.9% of government thought that more-effective debriefings for the losing bidders would reduce the frequency of protests.

More recommendations

Both government and industry want good and effective procurement, and everyone wants the government to get the best products or services at a good price. This is the underlying premise for best value procurements.

When we fail to accomplish this, we all lose. We are all in this together, and we can all succeed together. Better procurement is a win-win proposition.

There are many recommendations in the report with the data to substantiate them—download a copy (http://goo.gl/QYNtid).

WashingtonTechnology.com, October 16, 2014

Is price reasonableness really unreasonable?

With so many IT and professional services contracts being awarded to the lowest priced offeror, you have to wonder if the government is worried about awarding contracts to firms whose prices are unreasonably low.

As it turns out, in many procurements the government does not look for unreasonably low prices, and in some instances, is prohibited from doing so. In these procurements, low price has no floor.

The rules for examining price reasonableness and cost realism are complex and generally not well understood by capture and proposal professionals, so I thought I would point out some of the more interesting aspects of these rules about how low you can go.

Price reasonableness

Price reasonableness has nothing to do with low prices. Instead, it focuses on prices being too high. The government can assess price reasonableness by several methods—the most popular is comparing your bid prices to the prices of other bidders or comparing your prices to an independent government cost estimate (IGCE).

In both methods, the government looks at how high your bid is compared to the other bidders or the IGCE, and the amount of acceptable deviation is up to the contracting officer's discretion. In practice, the government tosses out very few bids for unreasonably high pricing because it is much easier in best value procurements to show that the high-priced offeror simply didn't provide the best value for the government when the source selection authority trades off cost and non-cost factors.

The question of price reasonableness being reasonable is really an inappropriate question since it only looks at the high side of pricing and doesn't examine the question of pricing being so low that it jeopardizes contract performance.

Looking at the low side of pricing is the realm of cost realism.

Cost realism in proposals for cost plus contracts

In cost reimbursable contracts, it is well established that the government is obligated to pay a contractor for actual and allowable costs incurred in the performance of the contract, not costs proposed by the contractor during the bidding process.

Because contractors tend to understate their costs when bidding, FAR 15.305(a)(1) and 15.404-1(d) require the government to review detailed cost information to determine whether the proposed costs are realistic and represent the costs that are likely to be incurred under the contractor's proposed technical approach.

This additional cost information can include a detailed breakout of direct labor rates, estimated hours, indirect rates, other direct costs, and profit. The government analyzes this information to determine whether the offeror's proposed costs demonstrate a reasonable understanding of the work to be done, are realistic, and are consistent with the technical approach proposed by the offeror. The contracting officer determines the level of analysis conducted; however, there is a requirement that this analysis must be done and the results documented in the contract file.

If the bid price is determined to be too low, the contracting officer has considerable discretion in what is done next.

Normally the bid price is adjusted upward to offset the unrealistic pricing, and in some cases, the technical score of the offeror can be lowered by showing that their unrealistic pricing demonstrates a lack of understanding of the work to be performed. The probable cost adjustment and the ability to down score the technical proposal act as a safety net to prevent awards from going to offerors with unrealistically low proposed costs on cost reimbursable contracts.

Cost realism in proposals for fixed price and time and materials contracts

FAR rules for cost realism analysis of price proposals for fixed price and time and materials

(T&M) contracts are simple. There aren't any. The logic here is that performance risk is borne by the contractor, not the government, and the contractor is obligated to perform the contracted work whether it underestimated its cost or not. Concerns over low price really become matters of offeror responsibility.

Smart buyers clearly see that the risk of poor performance is not entirely borne by the contractor since no government agency wants to be the recipient of impaired services provided by a contractor who can't pay prevailing wages or offer competitive benefits.

In these instances, the contracting officer must include language in the RFP that price proposals will be evaluated for cost realism to demonstrate that the contractor understands the work to be performed, the elements of costs are realistic, and the price is consistent with the offeror's proposed technical approach. With this language in the RFP, the government must conduct a cost realism analysis and document the results in the contract file.

Without language in the RFP specifically stating that the government will do a cost realism analysis, the government is prohibited from evaluating price proposals on the basis of cost realism, and to do so would be to evaluate a proposal using evaluation criteria that are not stated in the RFP. Clearly in this instance, fixed price and T&M contracts have no price floor, and it is impossible to disqualify a bidder based on lower, unrealistic pricing.

This has proven to be a fertile area for procurement protests since in many cases the government fails to do a reasonable cost realism analysis when it is required by the RFP or fails to document the results in the contract file. GAO reviews the government's records, and if the government did not document the cost realism analysis, the protest will be sustained.

Going a step further to prevent awards to unrealistically low-priced proposals

In addition to providing language in the RFP committing the government to conduct a cost realism analysis, the government can provide an extra measure of protection against unrealistically low-priced offers by requiring that the contractor submit a Professional Employee Compensation Plan with its proposal.

This requires the offeror to provide detailed analysis of its direct labor rates with details to substantiate that these rates are reasonable. Similarly, employee benefit details are examined to make sure pricing is sufficient to recover the cost of these benefits.

For non-exempt employees not covered by the Professional Employee Compensation Plan, the Service Contract Act can provide wage protection to prevent companies from proposing wage and benefits that are less than those determined by the Department of Labor in its Area Wage Determinations.

Including these additional requirements can help the government sidestep the pitfalls of awarding contracts to unrealistically low-priced offerors, but many government executives don't understand these rules or the consequences of awarding to an unrealistically low-priced offeror.

Summary

Price reasonableness and cost realism are very different concepts. The price analysis techniques under FAR 15.404-1(b) are for the purpose of establishing that the price is not too high—a fair and reasonable price—whereas the techniques for cost realism under FAR 15.404-1(d) are for the purpose of determining whether costs are too low.

Make sure you read your next RFP carefully to understand which tests the government intends to apply. You may be surprised to find that low price has no floor.

WashingtonTechnology.com, December 15, 2014

Killing bad capture and proposal habits

Instead of writing about all the things companies should do to be more successful in their business acquisition efforts, I thought I would lead off the year by writing about the things companies should stop doing.

Too many companies are stuck in the past with obsolete and ineffective practices that make their captures non-productive and proposals unnecessarily expensive. If you think this might apply to your company, then the first step for 2015 should be to drive out all the bad practices in order to make way for all the new practices you'll need to win.

Here's my list of some of the more egregious habits we've seen in companies. I hope that none of these apply to your firm, but just in case they do, make sure you put them on your kill list for 2015.

Capture management bad habits

1. Helter-skelter capture process

Don't go another year without defining your capture process, making it repeatable across all deals you pursue, managing every deal using your process without exception, and measuring how well you execute each step. The more consistently you execute the process, the better you will get at planning and executing winning capture campaigns.

2. No customer knowledge

Never underestimate the importance of customer knowledge and understanding. The bidder who understands the customer the best is most likely to win. Customer knowledge is so important that we make capture teams repeat daily the phrase, *best informed wins*. If you don't have any customer knowledge, then be realistic about your chance of winning, and make a good management decision and don't bid.

3. Lopsided call plan

Most call plans focus on the technical or program side of a government agency, but forget to include the contracting officer in the call plan. For many deals, you will want to visit the contracting officer to shape the procurement in your favor, if possible, and always remember this may be the person who is the source selection authority.

4. Delaying solution development

How many times have you heard the technical team say, "There is no RFP out, so how can we develop a solution?" This is just a way of dodging the need to do real solutioning work during capture. Doing it now lets you find out what you don't know and gives you time to validate your solution with the customer. If you don't start developing your solution during capture, you are running behind your competition.

5. Forgetting competitive analysis

Ignoring your competition leads you right into the trap where what you don't know gets you every time. Obsess about your competition—what you are going to do and how you are going to neutralize their strengths.

6. No price to win analysis

There is nothing more distressing than to realize you've worked for months pursuing a program and have made no progress in determining how to get to a winning price or even if you can. Don't ignore price to win. It has to be integral to your capture effort, and you need to base your analysis on real market data, not just management intuition.

7. Unvetted subcontractors

Ever have a subcontractor bring you a deal and then after you bid with them, you discover the customer hates them? It happens more often than you might think. I've never seen a subcontractor yet who doesn't say the customer loves them. Trust, but verify, is a good teaming practice to follow.

8. Waffling on resource commitments

Be in it to win, and pour on the resources when needed. Starving a capture effort resource-wise is a sure way to finish in second place or even further back in the loser list. Don't under-resource your capture efforts.

9. Bad bid decisions

Every technical team that reads an RFP and thinks they can do the work if awarded the contract wants to bid the job. The question to ask is not can we do the work, it is always, can we win. I still see companies bidding jobs because they want to do the work without a clue about what it takes to win. Will they ever learn that this is a losing practice?

10. No capture tools

Gone are the days when the only capture tool was a pad of paper. We now have capture tools that help automate the planning and execution of your capture campaign and integrate these activities with proposal development. If you are going to play in the major league of capture, you need to use these tools to their fullest.

Proposal bad habits

1. Late bid decisions

If you wait until the RFP has been out for 2 weeks to make your bid decision, then you are way behind the competition. Serious bidders have already done the capture work and are well along on their proposals. I know you are good, but most companies are not good enough to overcome this kind of competitive slow start.

2. Shifting proposal outlines

It seems so straightforward to build your proposal outline based on the information in the RFP, yet companies continue to change the outline with every review. Let's stop this practice of a meandering outline and, instead, assign experienced people to build and validate the proposal outline before you get started.

3. Writing without a solution

Inexperienced proposal teams often start writing without a solution, hoping that if they lay down enough text, a solution will emerge. Instead, most of this writing ends up in the shred box. Understand the solution before you write. It's the same in software development—design before you code.

4. Setting expectations for writers

More is not better. If you have three pages available to write your text and you come back with six, you haven't helped the effort. Similarly, handing in bullet charts instead of prose does not constitute a first draft. Be clear about expectations, and don't give anyone more time than they need to compose their first draft.

5. Skipping the editing process

If you think it's embarrassing to discover that the proposal you just submitted referred to your customer as the Navy when they are NASA, imagine how this affects the government evaluators. It certainly undermines all the statements you made in your proposal about how important this bid is to your company and how you understand the customer. A good editing pass across every proposal is essential if your goal is to present a professional bid.

6. Kill the storyboards

Storyboards seem to take on a life of their own and become speed bumps in the path of making good progress on proposals. Very few technical professionals can write effective proposal prose from storyboards. Kill the storyboards and replace them with annotated outlines, and quickly move from outlines to text. You will be much better off without the storyboards.

7. Color reviews that miss the mark

Most color reviews follow the proposal instructions with large groups of people sitting around the table wordsmithing the text. While no one doubts that the proposal must be compliant with the instructions, we must always remember that evaluators score proposals using the evaluation criteria. Always review your proposal from the point of view of the evaluation criteria, and see how many strengths you can find. You'll be amazed at how few strengths are actually observed in proposals and how poorly they will score without doing a strengths review.

8. Inadequate proposal training

With so much riding on how well you write proposals, you would think that everyone who is drafted to work on a proposal has gone through some training. More often than not, this is not the case. It's time to stop assigning inadequately trained people to write proposals and start insisting on some level of training and competency as a prerequisite to participating on a proposal team.

9. Misallocating proposal effort

Not all parts of a proposal are equally important, so allocate effort to the parts that evaluators will closely read and score. Allocate your effort and talent where the points are, and stop spending countless hours on sections of the proposal that aren't as important (while remembering to submit a compliant proposal).

10. Underutilized lessons learned

Follow every proposal submission with a lessons-learned exercise that involves everyone who participated in the capture and proposal efforts. If you are going to learn from each proposal experience, you will need to discover what worked well and what didn't. Make the review a learning experience, and stop relearning the same thing after each proposal.

Hopefully, you haven't seen any of these wayward practices in your company, but just in case you have, make note that you will need to drive these out of your culture if you are going to up your capture and proposal game in 2015.

WashingtonTechnology.com, January 7, 2015

Three strategies for growing in adjacent markets

Normally, the easiest way for government contractors to find new revenue is to prospect in adjacent markets, and the closer these markets are to your existing business base, the more successful you are likely to be.

Prospecting does not mean going around giving capability presentations to everyone in government who will listen. Instead, it is about figuring out how you can apply your company's expertise to help government leaders in adjacent markets be more successful in accomplishing their mission. Here are the guidelines that I like to use when following this strategy.

Set your market growth strategy

I like to set up a growth strategy as depicted in the following chart, which divides customers and sales offerings into four quadrants. Quadrant 1

represents your core business and core customers
and can be the easiest quadrant for growing new
business, especially if your current customers'
budgets are increasing.

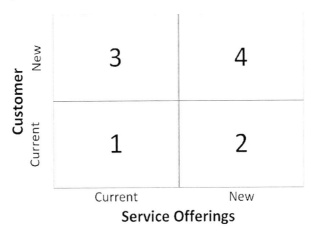

Quadrant 2 is the second easiest to sell into. It is
your current customers, but here you offer to sell
them new services or products. It is the second
easiest because you already have a trusted
relationship with these customers, contract
vehicles in place, and (presumably) you are doing
a good job for them. Often this quadrant is
referred to as the *up-selling quadrant* since you
are selling new services to your current customer
base.

The third quadrant is selling to new customers the same or similar services that you have been providing to other customers. This is the second most difficult quadrant to sell into since you don't have a trusted relationship or existing contract vehicles with these new customers. However, you do have a track record with past performance references.

The fourth quadrant is the most difficult quadrant because in this quadrant you are selling new services or products to new customers. Here, you don't have a track record and you don't have trusted relationships. When the battle cry for business expansion is *follow the money*, you will often end up in this quadrant.

Growing business with existing customers

The easiest path to business growth is to expand sales through satisfied, current customers so the first prerequisite to business growth is to do an outstanding job for your customers. Make sure you know how you really stand with them and make sure your company executives visit your customers to get an honest and independent assessment of how well you're really doing. Of course, if services are not meeting expectations, your first priority is to get performance back on track.

Your project/program managers or other customer-facing company executives who have responsibility for contract performance best handle growth in quadrants 1 and 2. Because your operations team understands the mission and challenges your current customers face, they should be able to explain how growing or adding new services or technologies can help your customers be more successful in accomplishing their mission.

As their current contractor, you have the *high ground* to see what your customer needs and access to explain how your company can help. Focus your discussion about your additional services on customer outcomes, and don't give a generic capability presentation. It is all about outcomes.

Unfortunately, many project managers have little or no training in BD and are reluctant to reach out to grow your company's share of the market they have at hand. Clearly, some BD training will go a long way toward making your project managers successful, especially if it is backed up by an incentive program that recognizes and rewards their accomplishments.

Train your project managers to understand that their most important task, aside from doing an outstanding job for the customer, is to be curious about the customer's mission and alert to opportunities to help or to solve problems. Don't hesitate to bring in another member of your company to offer help. Providing assistance from one of your subject matter experts or bringing in a company executive can go a long way here. Make sure you have a way to close a deal if your customer wants to buy. Closing might include adding work to your current contract, issuing a new task under a task order contract that you hold, using a GSA schedule, using a set-aside strategy, etc.

Growing business with new customers

Expansion into quadrants 3 and 4 begins with market research to identify agencies that plan to contract for work that is similar to the work you have performed previously. Pulling this data together is not too difficult since it is readily available from the government and from sources like Bloomberg Government (http://goo.gl/x3JDAe) and Deltek's GovWin IQ (http://goo.gl/9xHeiq). A list of government acquisition sources is also available on the APMP-NCA website (http://goo.gl/ySjm3R).

Use this data to help you focus your business expansion on the right government agencies. Most businesses don't have the resources to expand broadly across the government market, so you have to focus your expansion efforts carefully on selected agencies.

Once you've selected the agencies, the next step is to gain more understanding about the mission, programs, and people within the selected agencies because everything you are going to do to sell into these agencies should focus on how your firm can help them accomplish their mission.

When we do market strategy and pipeline development, we always package the results in three parts:

- The projects

- The people you need to talk to

- Your company's expertise relevant to their mission

The more you know about their mission and the better you understand the needs and desires of your prospective customer, the more successful you will be in selling into this quadrant.

Business developers usually lead the charge in this quadrant, but it doesn't have to be done by these people. If you have past customers who have moved to your target agencies, contact them. If you have program managers who have worked in these agencies previously, then follow those relationships to get some traction. Hiring former government executives from these agencies is another strategy. Hiring a consultant or teaming with companies who are already doing work for the target agency can get you started. There are multiple paths into an agency, and your mission is one of understanding and fact-finding.

Gaining business in quadrants 3 and 4 at some point will transition from prospecting for bid opportunities to pursuit once you find an opportunity that is a good fit for your firm. Pursuit should follow a rigorous process called *capture management,* and I have written about this process extensively in prior articles, including *20 BD habits to kill off in 2015* (http://goo.gl/fA0H7o) and *Six tips for building your new business pipeline* (http://goo.gl/KPWz9e).

If market expansion strategy puts you solidly in quadrant 4—new customers and new services— the best way to expand successfully is to buy another company that is already in this market and can provide your firm with a foundation for further growth. Most large businesses do strategic acquisitions just for this purpose because growing organically into these markets is too slow and too difficult without preferential contracting advantages that are offered to smaller businesses.

Putting It all together

To have a successful business expansion strategy, your operations team needs to be trained and focused on expansion in quadrants 1 and 2, your BD team needs to be focused on selected customers in quadrant 3, and your corporate development team needs to be working on acquisitions to expand in quadrant 4. If you are a pure play business developer and your company has assigned quadrant 4 to you, then recognize that you are working in the *missionary corner* of the quadrant. That is the quadrant where you spend your life walking around in the wilderness hoping to convert a few souls. You should probably dust off your resume because success in this quadrant without doing acquisitions is a long shot at best.

WashingtonTechnology.com, February 9, 2015

Acronyms Glossary

Acronym	Definition
APMP	Association of Proposal Management Professionals
BD	business development
BPA	blanket purchase agreement
CA	competitive assessment
CIO-SP3	Chief Information Officers Solutions and Partners contract
CO	contracting officer
DISA	Defense Information Systems Agency
DOD	Department of Defense
FAR	Federal Acquisition Regulations
FUD	fear, uncertainty, and doubt
GAO	Government Accountability Office
GSA	General Services Administration

Best Informed Wins

Volume 2 – Collected Articles of Bob Lohfeld
from *Washington Technology* (2013 – 2015)

Acronym	Definition
GWAC	government wide acquisition contract
HUB	Historically Underutilized Business
IDIQ	indefinite delivery/indefinite quantity
IGCE	independent government cost estimate
IT	information technology
ITES-2S	Army's Information Technology Enterprise Solutions Services contract
LPTA	lowest price technically acceptable
MAC	multiple award contract
MOBIS	Mission Oriented Business Integrated Services contract
NASA	National Aeronautics and Space Administration
NIH	National Institutes of Health
OCI	organizational conflict of interest
OPM	Office of Personnel Management

Best Informed Wins

Volume 2 – Collected Articles of Bob Lohfeld
from *Washington Technology* (2013 – 2015)

Acronym	Definition
PES	Professional Engineering Services contract
PTW	price to win
RFI	Request for Information
RFP	Request for Proposals
SDVOSB	Service Disabled Veteran Owned Small Businesses
SOW	statement of work
SSO	source selection official
T&M	time and materials
TMA	Training and Management Assistance contract
WOSB	Woman Owned Small Businesses